MORE WAL
CARI
AN⌐
NORTH CUMBRIA

37 CIRCULAR AND LINEAR WALKS

PUBLISHED BY THE CARLISLE & NORTH CUMBRIA GROUP OF THE RAMBLERS' ASSOCIATION

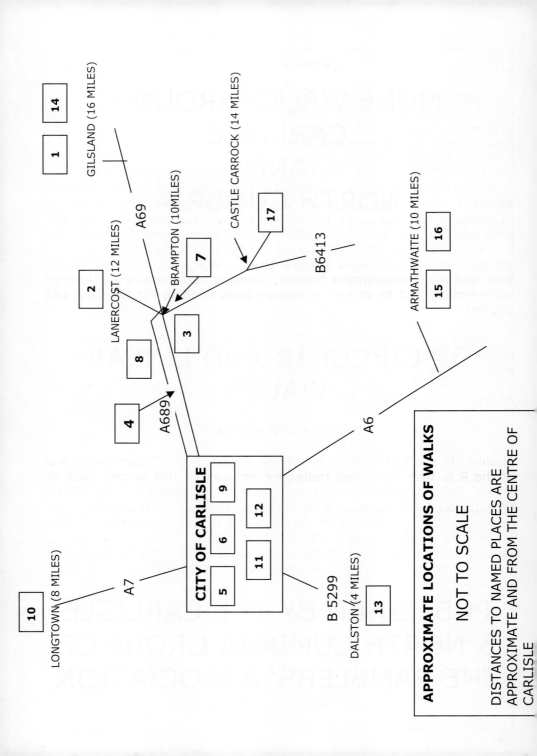

APPROXIMATE LOCATIONS OF WALKS

NOT TO SCALE

DISTANCES TO NAMED PLACES ARE APPROXIMATE AND FROM THE CENTRE OF CARLISLE

CITY OF CARLISLE

LONGTOWN (8 MILES)
A7
GILSLAND (16 MILES)
A69
LANERCOST (12 MILES)
BRAMPTON (10MILES)
CASTLE CARROCK (14 MILES)
A689
B6413
ARMATHWAITE (10 MILES)
A6
B 5299
DALSTON (4 MILES)

INTRODUCTION

As noted in introduction to our first book of walks, North Cumbria offers splendid and varied walking. To the West of Carlisle, a gentle land of pastures woods and hedgerows gives way to the marshes of the Solway Firth. To the East and North of the City are the wild fells of the Northern Pennines and the rolling border hills. The City is dominated by the beautiful River Eden, which comes up from the South and empties itself into the Firth. As you walk the routes in this book you will become aware of two major influences on the history and development of Carlisle and the surrounding area. Almost two thousand years ago the area was the northern frontier of the Roman Empire and Hadrian's Wall is the most visible reminder of that period. In the nineteenth century the coming of the railways brought about unimaginable changes to the area and many magnificent bridges, viaducts and massive earthworks were constructed to carry the railway lines heading for the City and beyond.

If, while enjoying these walks, you encounter problems of damaged stiles, or paths blocked by over adventurous vegetation, or deliberate action by landowners, please report the facts to the Ramblers Association at the address given in the preface. The information will be passed on to Local R.A. Officers.

ACKNOWLEDGEMENTS

Thanks are due to the members of The Carlisle & North Cumbria Group of the R.A. who suggested routes for inclusion in this second book of walks. Special mention must be made of Jo Leighton, who sifted through all the suggestions and compiled a list of interesting and varied walks. He then took on the huge task of walking all of the routes and preparing the initial draft of the directions. Thanks are due to Audrey Shore who produced the maps, Craig McNee who did the pen & ink sketches and Stan Benson and Bob Scanlan who did the proof reading.

Tony Iles.

Group Chairman.

THE COUNTRYSIDE CODE

Enjoy the countryside and respect it's life and work.

Be safe – plan ahead and follow any signs.

Leave gates and property as you find them.

Protect plants and animals and take your litter home with you.

Keep dogs under close control.

Keep to public paths across farmland.

Use gates and a stile to cross fences and walls.

The area covered by the walks in this book is one of mixed agriculture, including stock farming. Cows and steers often do not take kindly to dogs and there is a risk that they will run towards you. For reasons of safety, you are recommended not to take dogs with you. Also the period from January to April is the main lambing season and Ewes and lambs can easily be stressed by the presence of a dog.

If you do take a dog with you PLEASE KEEP IT ON A SHORT LEAD AT ALL TIMES when you are walking through enclosed pastureland. Sheep and lambs often shelter behind walls and are sometimes not immediately noticed.

The information in this book is provided in good faith and all reasonable efforts have been made to ensure that the details were correct at the time of publication. The publishers cannot accept responsibility for any errors or omissions. The maps are intended as guides to supplement the text. For more detail walkers are advised to refer to the appropriate 1:25 000 Ordnance Survey Map.

THE RAMBLERS' ASSOCIATION

The Ramblers' Association (R.A.) is a national organization that works to protect Britain's unique network of public rights of way and to defend the countryside by pressing for more effective planning controls to protect beautiful places.

The R.A. works with local authorities to resolve problems with illegally obstructed or overgrown footpaths.

Many thousand of miles of rights of way have been recorded and put on the definitive maps to ensure they are protected for future generations.

It has successfully campaigned for a legal right of access to some of the wildest and most beautiful parts of the country and seeks to enhance knowledge and respect for the countryside. Access to these areas of land will become available to walkers between September 2004 and November 2005. New Ordnance Survey maps showing access land will be published.

The next step will be to gain improved access to our coastline and beaches.

Although The R.A. is a national organization it functions through local groups up and down the country. These groups are run entirely by volunteers. Apart from the vital work on rights of way the groups encourage people of all ages to walk for health and pleasure by organizing programs of year round walks.

Details of membership can be obtained from:

The Ramblers' Association,
2nd Floor, Camelford House,
87-90 Albert Embankment,
London SE1 7TW

Web: www.ramblers.org.uk
Email: ramblers@londonramblers.org.uk
Tel: 020 7339 8500

CONTENTS

16. HIGH STAND

Two circular walks in the River Eden Valley
near Armathwaite.
8 or 9 miles (13 or 14km)

17. HEN HARRIERS & SPELTERS

Five circular walks on the Geltsdale Fells
starting from Jockey Shield.
3, 6.5, 10, 12 or 14 miles (5, 10, 16, 19 or 23km)

DISTANCES

The distances for each walk are as accurate as reasonably practical
and are rounded to the nearest 0.5 miles or 0.5 km.

Good walking shoes or boots are advisable on these walks.

Always take some waterproof clothing with you.

In winter, take extra clothing. Some of the routes can
be very exposed in poor weather conditions.

Ensure that you have adequate drink and food.

1. BRIDGE, FORT & STEPPING STONES

Three circular walks from Gilsland.

Distance:	3, 4 or 5.5 miles (5, 6.5 or 9km).
Map:	O.S. Outdoor Leisure Map. OL43 (Hadrian's Wall).
Start:	Front of Station Hotel, Gilsland. Grid ref: NY 637 663.
Parking:	Space in front of The Station Hotel, Gilsland.
	(The forecourt of a former busy railway station).

Note that an alternative starting point, car parking and information on the Roman Wall is available next to the school (see below).
(Grid reference: NY 631 663)

To do the 3 mile (5km) walk, head west, (to your left with the hotel at your back) following the signs to milecastle 48 at Poltross Burn on the Roman Wall. Do not follow the path under the railway but pause for a moment on the new footbridge to savour the view of Poltross Burn as it tumbles below the railway on its way to the River Irthing below. Climb the steps to the impressive ruins of the milecastle.
Equally interesting, is the small wood on the left bank of Poltross Burn. The wood, an example of the DEFRA Stewardship Scheme, is accessible from behind the milecastle and well worth a visit, particularly in spring when the floor is carpeted by bluebells.
Continue on the path along the railway line until you reach a stile. Cross the stile and the railway line, (look & listen!) and walk left across the field down to the road by the school (next to the car park). Cross the road to follow the signs for the Roman Wall Path and Willowford. The Wall and turrets along here are quite impressive. Note that the wall, just west of turret 48B, has tumbled into the River Irthing below. Pass Willow Farm and cross the river by the magnificent new bridge erected in 1999 to accommodate the Hadrian's Wall Path. The Romans also built a bridge here and the remains of its massive stone piers and a tower can still be seen. The path from the bridge leads up to milecastle 49 and the Roman fort at Birdoswald. Leave the fort and turn right, past the car park, to reach a finger post and stile on the right, which directs you across a field. Cross this field and the small, steep, wooded valley beyond, eventually reaching the road that runs from Gilsland to Langholm & Newcastleton. Turn right and continue along the road (there is no verge), until you reach a junction ('**A**'on

map). Turning to the right will return you to Gilsland, where, by following the road through the village and under the railway bridge you can return to your car at the Station Hotel car park.

To extend the walk to 4 miles (6.5km), go ahead at the junction ('**A**' on map), over the bridge and taking the next right fork past Orchard House on the left. A little further on another right fork takes you towards the

Gilsland Spa Hotel (the spa is still there and the waters available). Approaching the access road ('**B**' on map) to the hotel, a finger post directs you through a gate onto a field path that leads down to the River Irthing. The river, if not in spate, may be crossed on stepping-stones. The crossing is normally possible in the summer months. Turning right after the river crossing will return you to Gilsland, this time by the riverside path, to the road through the village and under the railway bridge to the Station Hotel car park.

To extend the walk to a longer and more interesting one of 5.5-miles (9km) continue up the access road ('**B**' on map) to the hotel and into the car park directly opposite the hotel entrance. A finger post at the top left hand corner directs you to a path down through the woods and into the River Irthing gorge. Here you will find the spa well and the sulphurous waters so attractive to the Victorians - we are told that bottling a sample and keeping it corked for a few weeks removes the sulphurous smell! Cross the river by the bridge and turn right to follow the path up through the wood to join the entrance drive to Wardrew House. At the drive turn right, eventually to join the unfenced road uphill and then downhill to where a finger post on the right directs you through a field to Irthing House. At Irthing House cross the road to the footpath opposite, between farm buildings and down to the footpath along the river to Gilsland and the Station Hotel car park. By ignoring the finger post leading to Irthing House and staying on the road you can walk directly into the village, but the riverside route is shorter, with no hills!

The walks all pass through Birdoswald Roman fort. A visit to the fort is a must. There is also a museum and visitor centre open from the 1st of March. The fort, in a prominent position overlooking the Irthing valley, guarded the River Irthing bridge and the northern approaches to the Roman wall. The Romans called the place Camboglanna and there have been suggestions that this is the site of the battle of 'Camlann' in which King Arthur died in 537 A.D.

1 BRIDGE, FORT & STEPPING STONES

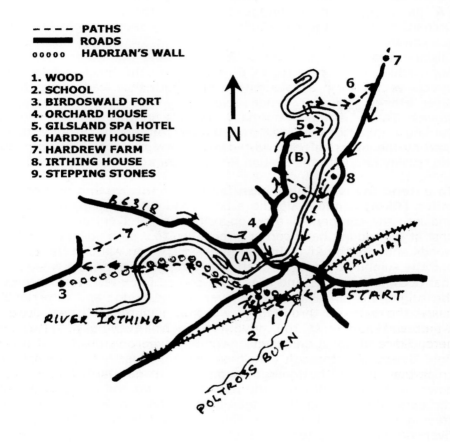

PATHS
ROADS
00000 **HADRIAN'S WALL**

1. WOOD
2. SCHOOL
3. BIRDOSWALD FORT
4. ORCHARD HOUSE
5. GILSLAND SPA HOTEL
6. HARDREW HOUSE
7. HARDREW FARM
8. IRTHING HOUSE
9. STEPPING STONES

2. A KING'S REST

Three circular walks from Lanercost.

Distance: 5, 6 or 6.5 miles. (8, 10 or 10.5km).
Map: O.S. Explorer No. 315 Carlisle.
Start: The old bridge at Lanercost. Grid Ref: NY 554 634.
Parking: Car park on north side of the old bridge at Lanercost.

Note that the turrets and milecastles mentioned are shown on the O.S. map, but they are unexcavated sites and not visible.

To do the 5 mile (8km) walk cross the road from the car park into the field opposite and follow the River Irthing eastwards to the Lanercost/Banks road and turn right. Follow the road and turn right into a narrow road signposted to Low Row, go over the bridge and continue to Crookstown and turn left into the lane beyond the farm. Follow the lane, then field paths and riverbank to the substantial farm bridge at Wallholme. Across the bridge there is a three finger sign post (right to Combe Wood, straight ahead to Banks Head and left to Banks hamlet). Take the path to the left, through the farm, along the riverbank and up the hill. On reaching the Lanercost to Birdoswald road at Banks turn left, then right at the road junction to reach the Lanercost to Roadhead road. Here turn left and after about 50 meters turn right into the lane leading to Hare Hill farm, and milecastle 53, passed on the right. A kissing gate in front of the farm gives access to a field and the footpath on the line of the Wall. Beware of soft ground here. Since leaving Banks you have been walking on The Hadrian's Wall National Trail, which runs from Wallsend in the East to Bowness on Solway in the West. Go past the sites of turrets 53A and 53B to reach Haytongate, ('**A**' on map) then turn left and take the track down to Lanercost and the car park.

To extend the walk to 6 miles (10km). At Haytongate ('**A**' on map), continue along the path, passing the site of milecastle 54, until you reach the next left turn ('**B**' on map) at Burtholme Beck. This path, which runs alongside and to the right of Abbey Gills Wood will return you to Lanercost. In springtime, the wood is carpeted with bluebells.

To extend the walk to 6.5 miles (10.5km).
Continue ahead from ('**B**' on map) through the fields, along the line of the Roman Wall, passing the site of turret 54A, until you reach the road from Lanercost to Walton ('**C**' on map). Here, turn left and walk downhill to Burtholme Farm buildings. Beyond the buildings, at Burtholme Bridge, a fingerpost on the right directs you through fields and along the riverbank to Lanercost Bridge and the car park.

KING EDWARD I MONUMENT-BURGH MARSH

The large medieval building to be seen across the road from the car park is Lanercost Priory. Largely ruined but with the nave beautifully restored and used as the parish church, the Priory is famous as one of the last resting places of Edward I. In the 14th century, Edward stayed here on his way to 'Hammer the Scots' but his departure was considerably delayed because of his illness. When the King finally left, he got only as far as Burgh Marsh near Sandsfield, on the edge of The Solway Firth, where he died on July 7th 1307. Detailed information about these events can be found inside the priory A monument marking the place of his death on the Marsh and the church in the nearby village of Burgh by Sands where he was laid in state, are well worth a visit.

2 A KING'S REST

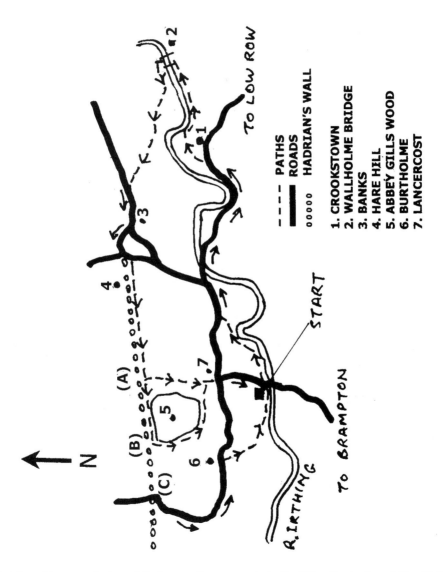

KEY

- - - - PATHS
━━━━ ROADS
ooooo HADRIAN'S WALL

1. CROOKSTOWN
2. WALLHOLME BRIDGE
3. BANKS
4. HARE HILL
5. ABBEY GILLS WOOD
6. BURTHOLME
7. LANCERCOST

TO LOW ROW

START

TO BRAMPTON

R. IRTHING

N

3. TARN & WOODS

Circular walk from Low Gelt Bridge.

Distance: 7.5 miles (12km).
Map: OS Explorer No 315 (Carlisle).
Start: Low Gelt Bridge, Grid Ref: NY 520 591.
Parking: Car park at Low Gelt Bridge. Limited roadside parking is possible with care.

Start from the car park at Low Gelt Bridge, which is just a short walk from the Carlisle to Brampton bus route. From here take the path through the woods uphill, avoiding the path to the right leading down to the river. When you reach the top of the hill, turn left at the signpost to 'Brampton' and very soon cross a stile on the right and head towards Unity. Continue along the path, which swings to the left just before the farm and eventually brings you to a 'T' junction. Here turn right and follow the path past Wreay to the Brampton to Castle Carrock road which you cross into the minor road ahead. Follow this road, over the railway (The Carlisle to Newcastle line) until you see a finger post on the right directing you to 'Talkin Tarn'. Take this path, keeping close to the field boundary on your right and cross the stile in the corner. Follow the path to the right and after a short distance, you will see the Tarn and the buildings of the Talkin Tarn Country Park, where there is a café, shop, toilets and information. Follow the path around the Tarn to the Tarn Hotel and fork right to join the road. Here turn left and walk along the road to the village of Talkin. At the crossroads go straight ahead and look for a signpost to 'Hill House' in the yard behind and to the right of the 'Blacksmiths Arms' pub. Climb the stone steps of the stile into the church grounds, following the yellow waymarks into the field. Cross to a prominent tree opposite then continue across the fields following the field boundaries on your right, to Hill House farmyard and onto a track that leads from the farm. Take this track until it bends to the right, then go straight ahead through a steel gate. Bear right across the field looking out for a signpost on the roadside. This is the same Brampton to Castle Carrock road that you crossed earlier.

Now turn right and walk along the road for 500 meters or so and enter a gate on the left, signposted to Greenwell. Follow this path and on nearing the house, walk to the left to a suspension footbridge crossing the river Gelt. The bridge is an interesting structure and rather shaky, so take it slowly and cross one at a time!   Cross the bridge and follow the pathway between the buildings of a converted mill to arrive at Greenwell hamlet. Here turn right and walk along the road for a short distance until you reach a footpath sign on your right, to Middle Gelt. Follow the riverside path until it reaches the road at the impressive railway viaduct at Middle Gelt Bridge. Go under the viaduct, turn right and take the path on the left into Gelt woods. After about 1.5km the path divides. Take the path leading downhill alongside the river and follow it to the car park. If conditions underfoot are unsuitable the upper path will also lead you back to the car park.

As you look at the beautiful countryside around Talkin, it is hard to realise that in the last decades of the eighteenth century, there was commercial extraction of coal from drift mines in the fells immediately to the South East of the village. In the early nineteenth century, shafts were sunk to get at the large reserves of coal close to Forest Head, about three miles to the East. The coalfield extended way beyond the immediate area and an extensive railway system was developed to handle the coal. The first steam locomotive to work on the system in 1837 was non other than the famous Stephson's 'Rocket'. Built in 1829 for the Rainhill trials on the Liverpool & Manchester Railway. 'Rocket' was much modified and altered by the time it appeared in the coalfield. Its working life was short and by 1840 it was ignominiously abandoned and put into store. Eventually, in 1862, it was given to the Patent Office Museum.

3 TARN & WOODS

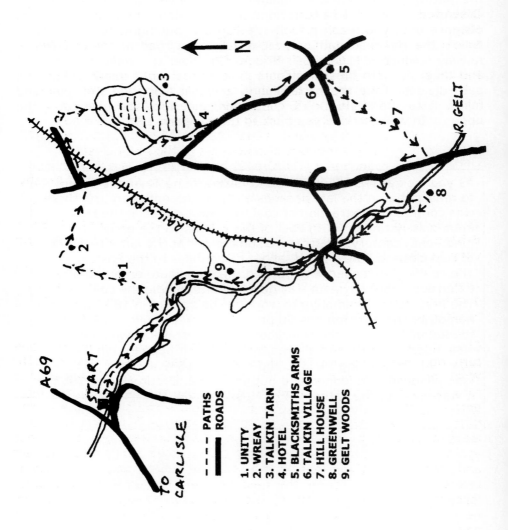

N

R. GELT

RAILWAY

A 69

START

TO CARLISLE

--- PATHS
— ROADS

1. UNITY
2. WREAY
3. TALKIN TARN
4. HOTEL
5. BLACKSMITHS ARMS
6. TALKIN VILLAGE
7. HILL HOUSE
8. GREENWELL
9. GELT WOODS

4. THE CROSBYS & SCALEBY

Circular walk from Crosby on Eden (High Crosby) via Scaleby Castle.

Distance: 8 miles (13km).
Map: O.S. Explorer 315 (Carlisle).
Start: Crosby on Eden at the Junction of Sandy lane and the A689, Grid Ref: NY 456 598.
Parking: It is possible to park in Low Crosby or Crosby on Eden (also known as High Crosby). To reach the start point, walk through Crosby on Eden to the A689. Parking is also possible on broad grass verges near the road junction of Sandy Lane with the A689 (Grid ref: NY 487 598). Parking is also possible at the A689 Linstock roundabout (Old Grove) but this involves a longish walk along the footpath/cycleway into Low Crosby and Crosby on Eden (High Crosby).

The right of way between Scaleby Castle and Brunstock Beck Bridge crosses former wetlands and can be waterlogged and very muddy, more especially in the winter months.

There is a regular bus service to the Crosbys. Bus times can be obtained from Carlisle Tourist Information Centre or by calling Stagecoach on 01946 63222.

Cross the A689 into Sandy Lane and walk down to the Military Way and turn right following the line of Hadrian's Wall. Follow the road to Wallhead and continue along the hard surfaced right of way until it turns left into Highfieldmoor Farm. Do not use the hard surfaced farm entrance, this is not a right of way, but follow the green lane to the farm. At Highfieldmoor Farm, enter the yard by a narrow gate and leave it by a farm gate ahead, immediately turning right, then right again until you reach a gate into a hard surfaced lane. Here turn left and continue until you reach the end of the second field on the right. Leave the lane and enter the next field via the gate and continue, following the way-marks along the bridleway, through gates, across fields and into the lane that meets the road at Mireside. Here turn left and walk the short distance along the road into Laversdale.

In Laversdale, find the inn on the left and turn into the signposted lane to Scaleby Mill. This lane can be muddy due to cattle and farm access traffic and the last 200m or so may sometimes be overgrown with vegetation. Turn right at the junction prior to Scaleby Mill. From the Mill continue to the road and here turn left for Scaleby, passing Fordsyke, High Hill and Scaleby Hall. At the road junction a little way beyond Scaleby Hall, turn left into the Scaleby Castle entrance drive and follow this lovely avenue of limes and other species of trees, to the Castle. The Castle is privately owned and special permission is needed to visit. Follow the right of way signs to the left of the Castle and continue along the bridleway, crossing the footbridge over Brunstock Beck eventually reaching the farm at Highfieldmoor, from where a short lane leads to the Military Way. Turn right and follow the Military Way past Wallhead, to Sandy Lane, which leads to the A689 and Crosby on Eden & Low Crosby.

A shorter circular walk is possible by turning right at Mireside, using the road for about 1km and rejoining The Hadrian's Wall Trail as it crosses the road. Here turn right and follow the bridleway back to Wallhead via Blea Tarn, Sandy Lane and the Crosbys

Crosby on Eden, as the name suggests is close by the River Eden. The river rises in Black Fell Moss on the high fells of Mallerstang Edge that towers above the eastern side of the valley that runs south from Kirkby Stephen to Garsdale. After tumbling over the gritstone edge it flows under the shadow of Wildboar Fell that dominates the western side of the valley. This magnificent river then runs in a generally northerly direction through wooded valleys, broad meadows, rolling hills, sandstone gorges, and villages and towns before it swings west to enter the Solway Firth and the Irish Sea. It dominates the area through which it runs and provides an effective barrier to travellers. As a result, there are magnificent stone built bridges in many locations, including the A66 trunk road.

4 THE CROSBYS & SCALEBY

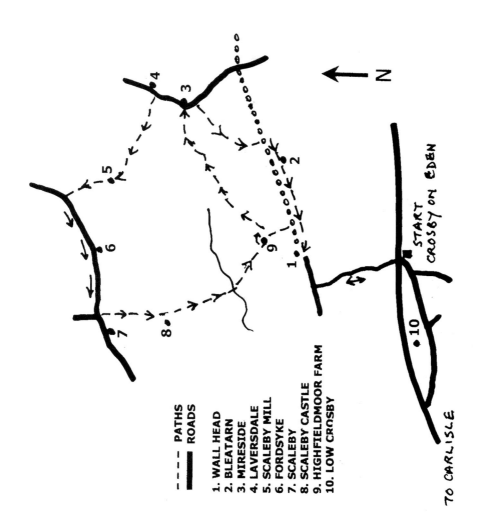

PATHS
ROADS

1. WALL HEAD
2. BLEATARN
3. MIRESIDE
4. LAVERSDALE
5. SCALEBY MILL
6. FORDSYKE
7. SCALEBY
8. SCALEBY CASTLE
9. HIGHFIELDMOOR FARM
10. LOW CROSBY

N

START
CROSBY ON EDEN

TO CARLISLE

5. BLEA TARN & OLD WALL

Linear walk from Carlisle to Irthington or Newtown, using The Hadrian's Wall Path – Return to Carlisle by bus).

Distance: 9 miles (14.5km).
Map: O.S. Explorer 315 (Carlisle).
Start: The Sands car park, Carlisle, Grid Ref: NY 402 565
Parking: The 'Sands Centre' Carlisle. (Off Hardwicke Circus, at the southern end of the River Eden bridge).

Bus times can be obtained from Carlisle Tourist Information Centre or by calling Stagecoach on 01946 63222. As routes and times vary, a bus timetable is strongly recommended.

Leave the Sands car park from near the Turf Inn; turn left to reach the riverbank and left again until you reach Eden Bridge. Do not use the underpass but go up the slope on the left on to the bridge. Cross the river and at the northern end of the bridge go down the steps into the ornamental gardens in Rickerby Park. Follow park footpaths or roadway until, passing the War Memorial on the right, you reach the footbridge, footpath and cycle way at the entrance to the park joining The Hadrian's Wall Trail. Continue ahead using path and roadway to the bridge over the motorway, cross the bridge and turn right into Linstock village. Take the right hand fork in the village and follow the road to the entrance of a farm lane signposted to 'Park Broom'. Follow the lane to a fork and take the lane ahead to Low Crosby. The entrance to this lane may occasionally have twine across it to assist the farmer with stock movement, just step over it. Continue to a 'T' junction of lanes and turn right towards the river. Follow the riverside footpath to where it ends at Greengate Head and join the road. Turn right then left to reach Crosby on Eden (also known as High Crosby). At the village turn right to reach the A689. **From here, you can catch buses to Carlisle.**

To continue the walk cross the road and go through the gate into Sandy Lane. At the end of the lane is the Roman Military Way on The Hadrian's Wall Trail. Here, turn right, passing Wallhead farm on the left. The right of way continues along a concrete roadway past a lane and a parallel farm entrance on the left and follows the line of

Hadrian's Wall, passing Bleatarn and Oldwall. Beyond Oldwall and Milecastle 59 is Chapel Field, a footpath crossroads. The bridleway on the right, which eventually becomes a footpath, leads to Irthington on a bus route to Carlisle. By continuing ahead from Chapel Field, you will reach Whiteflat from where the road straight ahead takes you to Newtown, which is also on the bus route to Carlisle.

Initially, the Roman wall in this area was twenty feet wide at the base and consisted of layered turf and the milecastles were of timber construction. The lime needed for the building of a stone wall could not be made locally due to a nearby geological feature known as the red rock fault. At the fault, limestone (necessary for lime production) gives way to red sandstone. After the urgency of the first period of wall construction between 122 and 126 AD, a much narrower stone wall gradually replaced the turf wall, which extended all the way to Bowness on Solway in the west. The timber milecastles were also replaced by stone structures. It is thought to have taken somewhere between thirty and forty years to finish the work. The water and reeds of Blea Tarn hide the remnants of a quarry that provided stone for this replacement wall.

As you look over the tarn the line of the Vallum lies behind the farmhouse. This massive earthwork, which lies south of the wall, originally consisted of a ditch ten feet deep and twenty feet wide at the top. It had sloping sides that lead down to a flat bottom that was eight feet wide. The excavated material was heaped up on each side to form continuous mounds thirty feet back from the edges of the ditch. The precise purpose of the Vallum is still unclear. The favoured view at present is that it was used to control the movement of people and goods across the frontier.

5 BLEA TARN & OLD WALL
CARLISLE TO CROSBY ON EDEN (HIGH CROSBY)

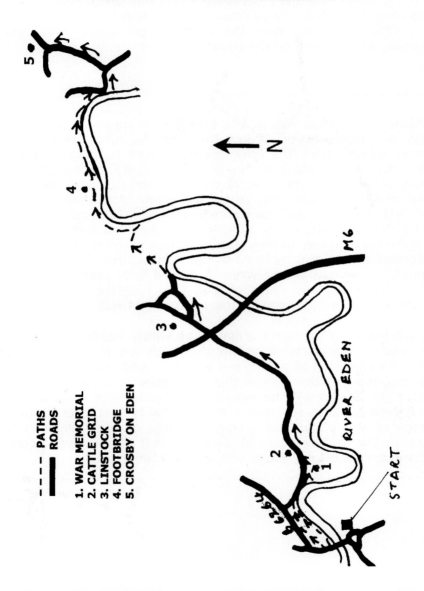

PATHS
ROADS

1. WAR MEMORIAL
2. CATTLE GRID
3. LINSTOCK
4. FOOTBRIDGE
5. CROSBY ON EDEN

5 BLEA TARN & OLD WALL

CROSBY ON EDEN (HIGH CROSBY) TO IRTHINGTON

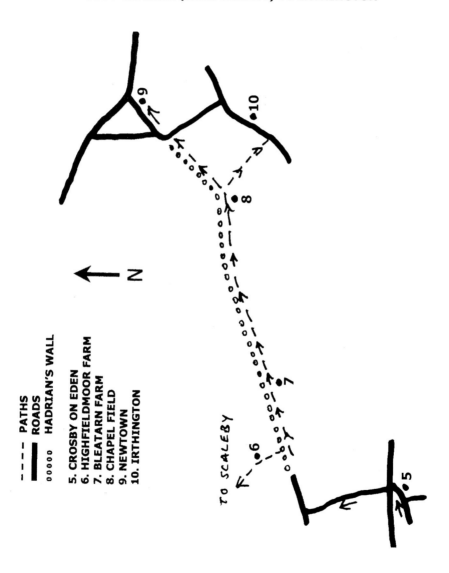

PATHS
ROADS
HADRIAN'S WALL

5. CROSBY ON EDEN
6. HIGHFIELDMOOR FARM
7. BLEATARN FARM
8. CHAPEL FIELD
9. NEWTOWN
10. IRTHINGTON

N

TO SCALEBY

6. COASTAL WAY.

Four linear walks along The River Eden from Carlisle to Rockliffe.
Return to Carlisle by bus from Rockliffe or Cargo.

Distance: 5, 7.5, 9 or 11 miles (9, 12, 15 or 17km).
Map: O.S. Explorer 315 (Carlisle).
Start: The 'Sands Centre' Carlisle. (Off Hardwicke Circus,
                  Grid Ref:NY 402 565. Opposite the Turf Inn.

Bus times can be obtained from Carlisle Tourist Information Centre or
by calling Stagecoach on 01946 63222. Please allow time to catch your
return bus, otherwise, you could have a long wait or a very long walk!
The bus stop in Carlisle is on West Tower Street opposite the indoor
market and a short walk to the left via the pedestrian underpass at
Hardwicke Circus will bring you to The Sands Centre.

To do the 5 mile (8km) walk leave the Sands car park from near the
Turf Inn, turn left, walk down to the river and follow the riverbank path
through the subway. Immediately on leaving the subway turn left up
some steps on to the River Eden Bridge. Cross the bridge and turn left
onto the path overlooking the cricket club and ski slope. Follow the
riverbank path, past the confluence with the River Caldew and the
avenue of fine crack willow trees to emerge on Etterby Scaur. At the
top of the hill, on the right, pass the former Nazareth House
Orphanage now Austin Friars public school and turn left into Etterby
Road.
The 'Redfern' pub you see just beyond the turn, is named after its
architect, Harry Redfern who is famous locally for the design of State
Management Scheme pubs.

Go down Etterby Road to the sign at the bottom directing you to the
River Eden. Follow the river downstream, passing below the sandstone
bridge that formerly carried the railway line of 'The Waverley Route'
from Carlisle, through the borders to Edinburgh. Across the river, is
the gleaming new Cumberland Infirmary. Now follow the way-marked
path crossing several metal stiles. Across the river is the village of
Grinsdale with its charming church partly hidden by trees.

Leave the riverside path by the second of two paths on the right ('**A**' on map) (both lead to Cargo). This second path leads to the road in the village, where the bus can be caught for the return to Carlisle.

To extend the walk to 7 miles (11 km), continue past path ('**A**' on map) and Cargo, following the long right hand bend in the river, past a small ruined building, and then a disused house. This was formerly the City of Carlisle Mayor's fishing lodge. Note the inscribed plaques on the rear wall- "George Pattinson 1751", "Joseph Polls 1780", & "Joseph Gill 1782". Approximately 200 meters past the house, turn right into a lane ('**B**' on map) that leads to Cargo and the bus for Carlisle. The village you can see on the other side of the river, as you follow the bend, is Beaumont.

To extend the walk to 9 miles (14.5km), continue past the lane ('**B**' on map) that leads to Cargo and follow the riverside path, go over the stile and after 250 meters, cross a small footbridge over a stream. The path then bears right towards electricity pylons and crosses another footbridge. Turn left and reach a more substantial footbridge in the corner. Bear left to rejoin the riverbank and another footbridge. This is the point where you will rejoin the river path on the short circular walk from Rockcliffe. Continue along the riverbank and at the end of the fence bear right and cross either of two bridges to join the road alongside the church in Rockliffe. This latter section of the riverbank has suffered from erosion, so take care. If you walk towards the river bank from here you will see the last of a series of 'Eden Benchmarks', a series of 10 sculptures situated at various points along the river from its source at Mallerstang to Rockliffe.
At the road junction – church on the left – you begin the circular walk round Rockliffe. This permissive walk around Rockliffe is the result of a DEFRA Stewardship Scheme grant to the Landowner and map/drawings are to be found at the various intersections.
The way turns left, (if you require refreshments then the Crown and Thistle pub is just along the road on the right). From the junction, walk down the slope and over the Rockliffe Bridge towards the minor road junction. Continue ahead towards Todhills. After the last house on the right turn into the lane. The lane turns right before the next gate (and pylon). Cross the stile keeping the hedge to your right. Cross another stile and pass along a short hedge lined path, then turn right in the field and left along the track to reach the road. To continue the

walk, cross the road with care and then go over the stile about 20 meters to the left. Walk with the hedge to your left and turn right in the corner of the field to eventually reach the Carlisle to Rockliffe road. Cross the stile and walk along the bank on the left for a few metres, to avoid the drainage ditch. To catch the bus from Rockliffe back to Carlisle turn right here ('**C**' on map) and return along the road to Rockliffe. The bus stop is Just past the road junction and on the right, opposite the Village Hall.

To extend the walk to 10.5 miles (17km). At the road ('**C**' on map), turn left for 150 meters and take another stile on the right to walk the permissive path. This leads you back to the river at the point mentioned earlier. Now turn left and cross the four footbridges crossed before and back to the head of the lane ('**B**' on map) leading back to Cargo, from where you can catch the bus back to Carlisle.

The salt marsh just to the west of Rockcliffe is the site of an ancient ford over the River Eden. In July 1307 King Edward I of England died of ill health close to the southern end of the crossing, thus putting an end to his plan to lead an army across the water to 'hammer the Scots'. Fortunes were reversed in 1745 when Bonnie Prince Charlie successfully led a large army across the ford into England, where he immediately laid siege to Carlisle and started his doomed attempt to seize the crown. Inevitably, the ford was also in regular use for cross border cattle rustling and whisky running. During the so called 'dark ages' the ford was in the kingdom of Rheged which included a good part of what is now Cumbria, part of Northumberland and land on the northern shore of the Solway. It is possible that it came into being as a spin off from the much larger kingdom of Strathclyde, which emerged after the final departure of the Romans sometime in the early fifth century. Under its great leader Urien it was one of the final bastions of resistance to the invading hordes from northern continental Europe. Legend has it that Urien became ruler of the kingdom following the death of King Arthur at the battle of Camlann in 537AD. Unlike Urien, Arthur is an enigmatic figure whose true identity remains a mystery.

6 COASTAL WAY

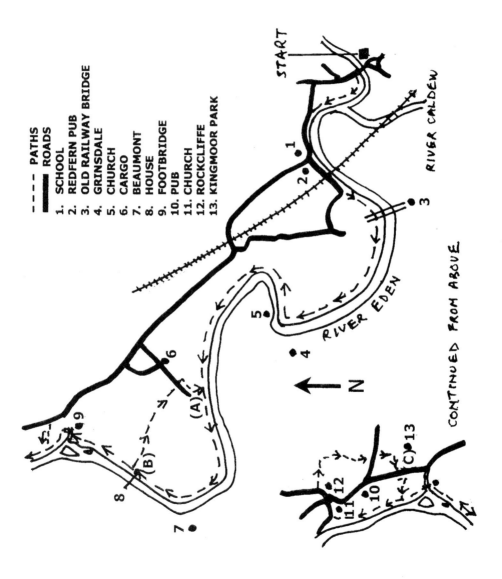

KEY
- - - PATHS
▬ ROADS

1. SCHOOL
2. REDFERN PUB
3. OLD RAILWAY BRIDGE
4. GRINSDALE
5. CHURCH
6. CARGO
7. BEAUMONT
8. HOUSE
9. FOOTBRIDGE
10. PUB
11. CHURCH
12. ROCKCLIFFE
13. KINGMOOR PARK

7. OLD CHURCH & ANCIENT PRIORY
Circular walk from Brampton

Distance: 9.5 miles (15km).
Map: O.S. Explorer No 315 (Carlisle).
Start: Off Longtown Road, Brampton. Grid Ref:NY 526 611.
Parking: Any suitable place in Brampton.

As an alternative to using your car, you can reach Brampton by using the regular bus service from Carlisle. Bus times can be obtained from Carlisle Tourist Information Centre or by calling Stagecoach on 01946 63222. As routes and times vary, a bus timetable is strongly recommended.

Leave Brampton by the Longtown road and after 200 meters a finger post on the left directs you onto a footpath behind an industrial complex leading to 'The Old Church'. On reaching Old Church Lane turn left and continue until a fingerpost on the right 'Crooked Holme,' is reached.
The Old Church is medieval and was built with stones from a Roman fort on 'Stanegate' and is well worth a visit. It is a few hundred metres further along the road.
Cross the stile for Crooked Home and follow the hedge, crossing further stiles and passing an old firing range on the left. Continue past Crooked Holme on the left, to join a lane leading right, which brings you to the Brampton/Longtown road. Turn left and follow the road to the bridge across the River Irthing. A little distance after crossing the bridge, take the minor road to the right and after 100 meters cross a stile on the left. This right of way crosses a large field with a stile halfway
(Castlesteads house can be seen on your left). Aim for the top right hand edge of a wood, which can be seen at the top of the field. On reaching the gate at the edge of the wood turn right and follow a track leading to Sandysike. At Sandysike take the track on the right, alongside the farm buildings and as you leave it, pass through an open gateway, to join The Hadrian's Wall Path. From here follow the Acorn waymarks through Walton (alternative starting point), noting that you pass The 'Centurion Arms' pub. Continue along the signposted Lanercost road to Dovecote Bridge, which takes the road over King

where on the right you will see a gate and sign for The Hadrian's Wall Path.

Note: At the time of publication, The Hadrian's Wall Path followed the road from Dovecote Bridge to this gate. This is a temporary route pending the provision of a new footpath through the fields on the left hand side of the road. Access to this new path should be immediately on your left, as you leave the bridge. Look out for The Hadrian's Wall Path signs and acorn symbol. This will enable you to reach the gate without walking along the road.

The path leaving the road at this gate is one of the new paths created especially for the Hadrian's Wall Trail and is not currently marked on the O.S. Map 315. Go through the gate and follow the waymarks until you meet the road again. At the road turn right for a short distance and then left at the finger post to continue along The Hadrian's Wall Path. Follow the waymarked path across stiles and a footbridge until a farm approach road appears. Here, turn right to leave The Hadrian's Wall Path and go down the side of Abbey Gills Wood. The wood on your left is renowned for its Bluebells, which in spring attract many visitors. At the bottom of the track turn left along the highway.

At this point, you will see the partially restored ruins of Lanercost Priory. A visit to the Priory is a 'must'. (see notes to walk 2 - 'A King's Rest').

After 200 meters or so, go through a gate on your right leading to the Priory and follow the field hedge to another gate on your left. Go through the gate and follow the path right, then cross a stile and walk across the field to the riverbank. Turn right along the river to the stile at the road.

Now turn left to cross the River Irthing and after a short distance take the minor road to the left signposted to Naworth. Go up the hill and after about 100 meters take a footpath on the right, signposted 'Brampton via Quarry Beck'. After 1km this path meets the road, which you cross to follow the road towards Easby. After about 300 meters turn left up a track signposted 'Brampton via the Ridge'. After another 300 meters go over a stile on the left and climb up the hill towards the wood. Look out for the `Woodlands Trust` sign welcoming walkers to the woods. Follow the path along the ridge. Look out for a seat that is moulded around a tree and sit for a while to enjoy the view northwards encompassing the route of most of this walk. A stile will take you out of the wood and the path continues in the same direction towards Brampton, now clearly in view. This path descends to the Lanercost/Brampton road at the Sands where you turn right for Brampton town centre.

GATEWAY TO LANERCOST PRIORY

7 OLD CHURCH & ANCIENT PRIORY

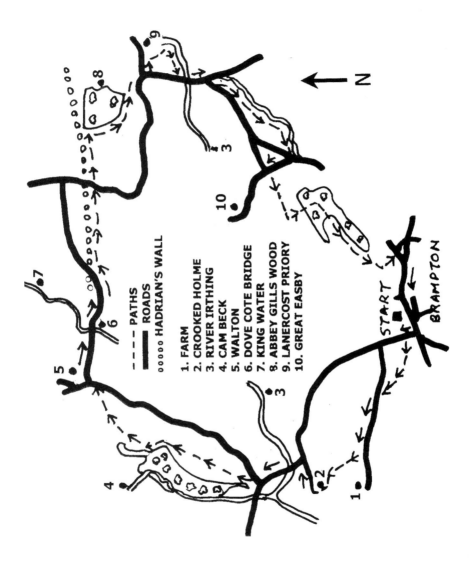

Reproduced by permission of Ordnance Survey on behalf of The Controller of Her Majesty's Stationary Office, © Crown Copyright 100033886

8. THE CONSERVATIONIST.

Circular walk on permissive paths at Hollinstone.
(A DEFRA Stewardship Scheme).

Distance: 3 miles (5km).
Map: O.S. Explorer 315 (Carlisle).
Start: Stile next to notice board on the ...... east of the bridge over the River Irthing 494 603
Parking: At Ruleholme on the A689 ...... Brampton road), turn left ...... the Golden Fleece inn. Go past the ...... the road verge beyond the ...... River Irthing.

This walk ...... west Cumbria Countryside Project in co-operation with ...... Owner/Farmer and DEFRA under the Countryside Stewardship Scheme. Note that the agreement may be terminated after 10 years.

There is a regular bus service along the A689 from Carlisle to Brampton. The bus stop for this walk is Ruleholme. Bus times can be obtained from Carlisle Tourist Information Centre or by calling Stagecoach on 01946 63222.

Walk along the road to a notice board on the right, which gives you information on the walk. Cross the stile into a small field and keeping to the left, pass beneath the road bridge crossing the River Irthing. Follow the river around the large bend and notice the confluence of the two rivers, Gelt and Irthing. With its wild life and native trees, the river is a delight to walk along. You may see the flash of a kingfisher or, in spring and early summer, sand martins feeding young in holes in the riverbank. Cross the stile into the wood where you may hear or see woodpeckers and squirrels and where there is an abundance of ground covering woodland plants. Follow the riverbank, eventually leaving the wood. Continue along the edge of the field, past an electricity pylon and join a line of trees along the riverbank. Presently, leave the river and turn left to cross the fields towards the A689-using the field boundaries as a guide. At the bottom of the last field approaching the road, made damp by a beck, is a "Set-aside" patch where exotic seed bearing plants are grown for feeding raised pheasants as well as wild birds such as finches.

Walk 8 – The Conservationist. This walk was subject to an agreement under the Countryside Stewardship Scheme. This agreement has now expired so this walk is no longer available. The agreement may be renewed in due course. June 2008.

At the road, turn right for a few metres until the stile is reached and here cross the road with great care. Cross the stile at the other side and follow the path to the top of the field into a small wood. On the other side of the wood follow the path down into the field and join the riverbank. Here turn left to follow the river to the stile at the bridge where your car is parked.

The dictionary defines the word 'conservation' as 'keeping from harm, decay or loss' and in this sense farmers have from time immemorial been conserving their land and animals. The practical means of doing so have of course changed over time. There are vast numbers of sheep in Cumbria and it is interesting to consider how farmers protected their flocks from various diseases and parasites before the advent of modern veterinary practice. The twice yearly dipping of sheep to prevent parasite attack involved the use of some rather novel and in some cases dangerous and toxic substances. Arsenious acid (a compound of arsenic), sulphur, washing soda, tobacco extract and caustic soda mixed in varying proportions with soft soap and water was commonly used. The use of carbolic acid (phenol) and pitch oil was however frowned upon by the wool merchants. To treat foot rot (which can affect sheep pastured in wet conditions) the sheep were walked through quicklime, phenol or copper sulphate! Attack by maggots could be treated by the application of paraffin, turpentine and rapeseed oil to the affected parts and scab was dealt with by the use (amongst other things) of mercury compounds. In times past, wool was a valued commodity and farmers had to be careful not to overdo some of these treatments and reduce the value of the wool. In the late 19th century The Bradford Wool Buyers Association issued guidelines on the washing of sheep before clipping. There was also a rather amusing guideline regarding the weighing of wool. It was suggested that weighing at railway stations was best avoided since the railway companies were only interested in the weight for freight charging purposes and the weight was sometime a bit of an approximation!

8 THE CONSERVATIONIST

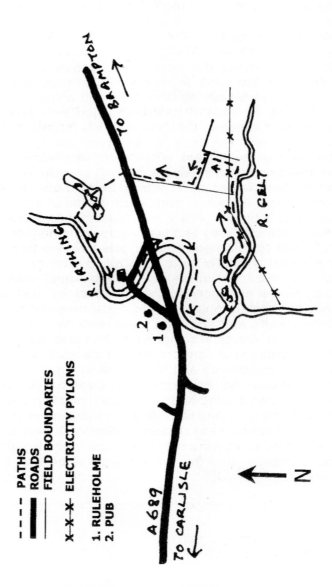

TO BRAMPTON

R. GELT

R. IRTHING

A689

TO CARLISLE

PATHS
ROADS
FIELD BOUNDARIES
x—x— ELECTRICITY PYLONS

1. RULEHOLME
2. PUB

N

9. THE MEANDERING EDEN

Three linear walks from Carlisle to Scotby, Warwick-on-Eden or Wetheral.

Return by bus from Scotby, Warwick on Eden or Wetheral.
Return by train from Wetheral only.

Distance: 5, 8 & 8 miles (8, 13 & 13km).
Map: O.S. Explorer 315 (Carlisle).
Start: The Sands Centre car park off Hardwicke Circus, Carlisle-opposite the Turf Inn. Grid Ref: NY 402 565.

Bus times can be obtained from Carlisle Tourist Information Centre or by calling Stagecoach on 01946 63222. Rail information can be obtained from Carlisle Railway station or by calling National Rail inquiries on 0845 484950.

To do the 5 mile (8 km) walk leave the car park by turning left at the Turf Tavern to join the riverside path. Turn right and follow the riverside path to the Memorial Bridge, but do not cross. Go ahead and cross the River Petteril Bridge at the confluence of the two rivers and continue along the riverside path, with the golf course on your right, for about 2km until a gate into a lane (Johnny Bulldog's Lonning) is reached. Who was Johnny Bulldog? No one seems to know! Enter the lane and continue along the riverbank. The course of the river here has changed considerably in recent years and with it the footpath. Take care.

Follow the riverbank below the motorway and around the first sharp bend. It is well worth sitting for a while on the bank of this quiet stretch of the river to observe the many species of water birds that make the river their home-particularly in the winter months. Leave the river at the next bend and join Holme Lane leading to the main road, Scotby road end and Wheelbarrow Hall Farm. The lane is not a public right of way but at the time of writing, access is allowed by kind permission of the landowner. The bus stop (and bus shelter) for the bus back to Carlisle can be seen across the main road ('**A**' on map).

For a longer walk, you can return on foot by turning right and crossing the motorway intersection. Pass the Tesco supermarket and immediately turn right into Johnny Bulldog's Lonning to follow the riverbank back to the city centre or continue along the road (Warwick Road) to the City centre.

To extend the walk to 8 miles (13km) cross the dual carriageway road ('**A**' on map) and walk into Scotby village eventually passing under the railway bridge (Settle & Carlisle line), past the Church on the left and the Post Office further along on the right. Turn left down the Wetheral road and continue, using grass verges, for about ¾ of a mile then turn into a lane on the left ('**B**' on map). (Do not turn into the first lane on the left just beyond Beck House- this goes to Warwick-on-Eden – see below) and shortly cross the railway line with great care. Follow the lane past the golf course and approximately 200 meters before the lane reaches the road turn right into the field. At the top left hand corner of the field re-cross the railway line again, taking great care. Join the lane on the other side and follow it into Wetheral village. The return to Carlisle may be by rail or bus.
Check the bus timetable at the bus stop at the Green and be aware that alternate services use different routes and note too that not all Newcastle/Carlisle trains stop at Wetheral.

An alternative linear walk of 8 miles (13km) takes you to Warwick on Eden from where bus transport is available into Carlisle – the bus stop is on the main road. To do this, walk through Scotby under the railway bridge past the Church and Post Office further along. Take the Wetheral road off to the left and walk along for approximately ¼ of a mile and enter a lane ('**C**' on map) on the left under the railway. At a gate turn right and follow the paths across the fields into Carlisle golf course. Follow the marked posts through the course. It is a right of way but take great care when crossing the fairways and please show courtesy to golfers who may be playing through. From the golf course follow the path through Warwick Moor Wood, across Wetheral Plains road and into the field opposite. Follow the path past Moorhouse Farm and Moorhouse Hall and into the car park of the Queens Arms Inn.

9 THE MEANDERING EDEN
CARLISLE TO SCOTBY

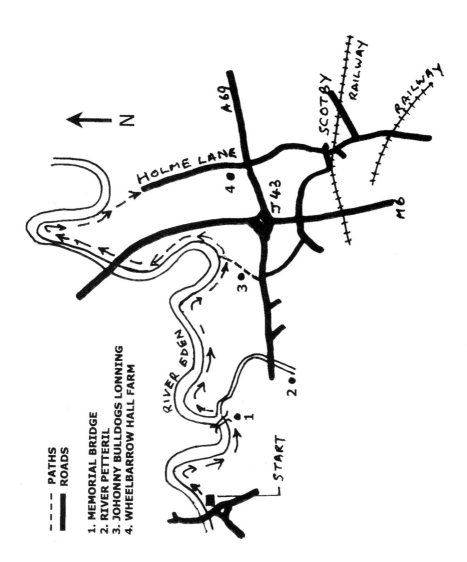

PATHS
ROADS

1. MEMORIAL BRIDGE
2. RIVER PETTERIL
3. JOHONNY BULLDOGS LONNING
4. WHEELBARROW HALL FARM

9 THE MEANDERING EDEN

SCOTBY TO WARWICK ON EDEN & WETHERAL

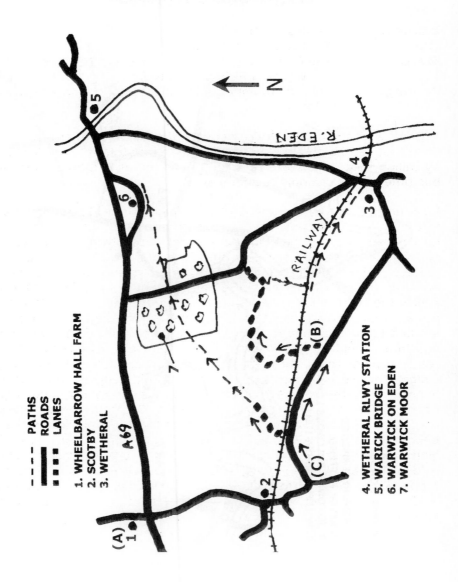

PATHS
ROADS
LANES

1. WHEELBARROW HALL FARM
2. SCOTBY
3. WETHERAL

4. WETHERAL RLWY STATION
5. WARICK BRIDGE
6. WARWICK ON EDEN
7. WARWICK MOOR

R. EDEN

RAILWAY

A69

10. ENGLAND'S LAST TOWN

Circular walk round Longtown

Distance: 5.5 miles (9km).
Map: O.S. Explorer 315 (Carlisle).
Start: At the Community Centre at the south (Carlisle) end of
The town. Grid Ref: NY 380 685.
Parking: At the Community Centre at the south (Carlisle) end of
The town.

There is a frequent bus service between Carlisle and Longtown.
Bus times can be obtained from Carlisle Tourist Information Centre or
by calling Stagecoach on 01946 63222. As routes and times vary, a
bus timetable is strongly recommended.

Walk north from the Community Centre along the wide tree lined street
to the bridge over the River Esk, but do not cross.   At the right hand,
upstream corner of the bridge take the steps down to the riverbank
and follow the path to the Pow Burn to join the Netherby Road at Pow
Bridge.   Follow the road for about 200 meters then take the last lane
on your right (before the open fields) leading to a housing estate.
Follow the hard surface road around the perimeter of the estate to join
a main road, leading east out of the centre of Longtown.   Here, turn
left and follow the road for about 200 meters until a finger post directs
you into a field on your right.   Follow the field boundaries until you
reach a minor road. Turn left onto the road and follow it past Virginia
Lodge (The old Isolation Hospital - now an old peoples home) to a left
hand bend.   After a very short distance, take the road to your right to
Brisco Hill Bridge on the A6071 Longtown to Brampton road.   Cross the
road where a finger post directs you into the field and follow the field
boundary to the A7 Longtown to Carlisle road. Hall Burn flows
alongside the path for part of the way and where it turns left there is
evidence of an old lead mine. Cross the Carlisle to Longtown road into
the field opposite and follow the field boundary until you reach a minor
road.   Here turn left, pausing to look at Faulds Mill and the nearby St
Michael's well.

In former days Longtown folk ground their corn at the mill with the equipment supplied by the Lords of the Manor – The Grahams of Netherby - the tenants paying for the upkeep of the mill.
Continue on the road to the entrance to the Arthuret church.

Return to the road, walk south until a fork is reached and bear right. Shortly you will cross the track bed of the dismantled 'Waverley Route' railway line that ran between Carlisle to Edinburgh (1862-1969).
Walk on to 'The Fauld' farm and enter the farmyard and follow the sign to 'The River'. At the farm, notice the circular 'gin', where prior to the advent of steam, horses were harnessed to a beam to provide power to the threshing mill.
Follow the lane to the River Esk – famous for sea trout angling - turn right and follow the path. The ponds on the left are flooded gravel pits, now a bird sanctuary. Do not enter the town but continue along the riverbank to Esk Bridge noting the information board on the riverbank. Complete the walk by following the path up between cottage gardens. Turn right at the main street for the return to the Community Centre.

The design of the magnificent five arch Bridge over the River Esk, The Graham Arms Hotel and the layout of the town were the work of Dr Robert Graham in the mid 1700's. The Graham Arms, originally known as the New Inn, was probably the town's dominant coaching Inn. Two other coaching Inns survive under their original names- The Bush Inn and The Globe Tavern. From The Globe, coaches left for Edinburgh at 5 a.m. on Mondays, Wednesdays and Fridays; and for Carlisle at 4p.m on Tuesdays, Thursdays and Saturdays. Over the centuries, there have been claims of a connection between the town, Arthuret church and King Arthur. It has been suggested that the name 'Arthuret' is derived directly from that of the King and that in the 6th century two battles took place nearby. One battle is claimed to have cost 80,000 lives and the other is said to have involved Merlin, who afterwards went insane and wandered the countryside for decades. It is highly likely that in the century following the final break up of the Roman Empire, there was a powerful leader or 'King' in the area, but the legend of King Arthur remains shrouded in mystery.

10 ENGLANDS LAST TOWN

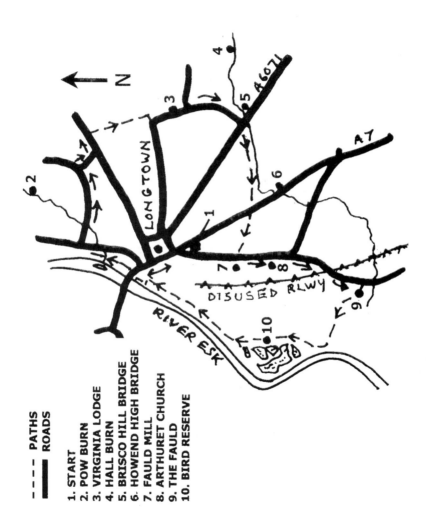

PATHS
ROADS

1. START
2. POW BURN
3. VIRGINIA LODGE
4. HALL BURN
5. BRISCO HILL BRIDGE
6. HOWEND HIGH BRIDGE
7. FAULD MILL
8. ARTHURET CHURCH
9. THE FAULD
10. BIRD RESERVE

11. TWO RIVERS

Two circular walks in The City of Carlisle along the River Eden & the River Caldew.

Distance: 3 or 7 miles (5 or 11km).
Map: Explorer 315 (Carlisle).
Start: The Sands Centre car park off Hardwicke Circus, Carlisle, Grid Ref: NY 402 565.
Parking: The Sands car park, opposite the Turf Inn.

To do the 3 mile (5km) walk leave the car park by turning left at the Turf Tavern to join the riverside footpath towards the Eden Bridge. Before the underpass, walk left up the slope to join the bridge. Cross the river and enter the ornamental gardens on the right and follow the footpath in Rickerby Park until you reach a rising path on the left.

Follow the path up to join Brampton Road. Turn right and follow the road to Well Lane. Here, cross the road and walk up to the top of Well Lane then turn right into Tarraby Lane where you will see the fine modern buildings of The Cumbria Institute For The Arts. At the point where Tarraby Lane goes left into Beechwood Avenue go straight ahead into the lane signposted to Tarraby. You are now walking along an ancient way, its age can be judged by the number and variety of plants, trees and bushes lining it. Tarraby Lane sits on the line of Hadrian's Wall. Follow the lane into a field and after a short distance turn right into another field leading to Brampton Road. Cross the road with care and go down Longlands Road into the housing estate. Continue ahead and cross the road into a short lane between two houses and through the wooden gate into a field. Turn half right and follow the direction of the fingerpost to the entrance to Rickerby Park, where there is a cattle grid and footbridge. The footbridge and the cycle path by-passing the village of Rickerby were built to accommodate the Hadrian's Wall Path. Cross the Park entrance road and take the path ahead indicated by the Hadrian's Wall Path waymark (National Trail acorns). The route takes you alongside Brunstock Beck, then the River Eden, to the Memorial Bridge. Cross the bridge and at the other side turn right and follow acorn waymarks along the riverside path until you reach Eden Bridge and The Sands Centre.

For the 7 mile (11km) walk leave the car park by turning left at the Turf Inn to join the riverside footpath towards the Eden Bridge, go through the underpass and walk ahead through Victoria Park, until you reach the tennis courts. In the spring and summer the park is ablaze with colour from the shrubs, trees and flowerbeds. Note Queen Victoria's statue in the centre.

Now turn right down the side of the tennis courts and follow the tree lined roadway as far as the bridge crossing the River Caldew.
As you near the bridge look to the right and you will see amid the trees, Carlisle's "Eden Benchmark", one of a series of sculptures along the banks of the river Eden that "Celebrate a very special river".
A little further on, again on the right, is the confluence of the two rivers. Do not cross the bridge but follow the road left until you reach the Castle and bear right to eventually join Castle Way. Cross by the Millennium Bridge and admire the view over the City. When you reach the bottom of the steps, go left and under the bridge, then immediately after the road crosses the West Coast Main railway line go left into Viaduct Estate Road down the hill towards the Carlisle Bridge Club building, here turn right to join the Caldew riverside path.
This part of the path, rescued from a disused rail line, crosses the River Caldew for the first time on the walk. As you walk along, look left and admire the line of the Cathedral and the mediaeval city walls.
When the path ends, continue to the end of the street and turn right then left into Denton Street. Continue and take the first left turn into Metcalfe Street and at the end rejoin the Riverside Path. Follow the path, passing two footbridges (do not cross either of these), and go past the weir at Holme Head, where at certain times of the year you can watch salmon leaping. Walk along the riverbank or the cycleway to Cummersdale. At the factory gate, cross the river by the footbridge (The factory, owned by the Lewis Partnership, is a world famous fabric printing works).
After crossing the bridge, turn left to follow the river back past the weir to the Grassing footbridge. Cross the bridge to rejoin the Caldew Riverside Trail and retrace your steps over the Millennium Bridge to the Castle, Victoria Park and the Sands Centre Car Park.
These walks can of course be combined to give a walk of 10 miles (16km).

An interesting variation of the walk can be done by heading for Blackwell, on the footpath that goes straight ahead at the end of the bridge at the factory in Cummersdale. This path goes through a railway underpass and joins the farm lane past Black Hall Farm to the White Ox Pub at Blackwell from where you can catch a bus back to the City centre. The distance from the bridge near the factory to Blackwell is about ¾ of a mile.

This walk can also be done in parts by returning to the City Centre by bus. Bus services can be joined at:
Brampton road, Denton Street and Cummersdale Village. (To reach the Cummersdale village bus stop, follow the road away from the factory gate and uphill to the village.)

Bus times can be obtained from Carlisle Tourist Information Centre or by calling Stagecoach on 01946 63222. As routes and times vary, a bus timetable is strongly recommended.

CARLISLE CASTLE

11 TWO RIVERS
EXTENSION TO CUMMERSDALE

FOR ROUTE DIRECTIONS WITHIN THE CITY OF CARLISLE REFER TO TEXT

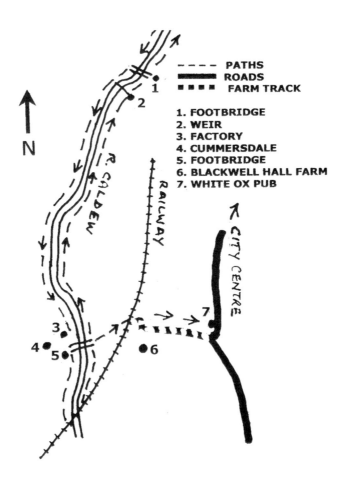

- - - - PATHS
▬▬▬ ROADS
■ ■ ■ ■ FARM TRACK

1. FOOTBRIDGE
2. WEIR
3. FACTORY
4. CUMMERSDALE
5. FOOTBRIDGE
6. BLACKWELL HALL FARM
7. WHITE OX PUB

12. CLYDESDALES & LOCO'S

Two circular walks north of the River Eden in Carlisle.

Distance: Both walks 7 miles (11km).
Map: O.S. Explorer 315 (Carlisle).
Start: The Sands Centre car park off Hardwicke Circus, Carlisle, opposite the Turf Inn. Grid Ref: NY 402 565.
Parking: The Sands car park.

To do the first 7 mile (11km) walk, Leave the Sands car park near the Turf Inn. Turn left to reach the riverbank and left again until you reach Eden Bridge. Do not use the underpass but go up the slope on the left onto the bridge. Cross the river and at the northern end of the bridge go down the steps into the ornamental gardens and take the path through the park until you reach a rising path on the left; follow it up to join Brampton road. Turn right and follow the road to Well Lane. Here, cross the road and walk up to the top of Well lane then turn right into Tarraby Lane where you will see the fine modern buildings of The Cumbria Institute For The Arts. At the end of the road, go into the green lane (which is a continuation of Tarraby lane) signposted to Tarraby.

You are now walking along an ancient way that sits on the line of Hadrian's Wall. The number and variety of plants, trees and bushes on each side is a measure of its age.

Follow the lane into and across the fields beyond into Tarraby village, famous as the home of the Clydesdale Stud (see the plaque on the wall of the farm-like building on the right).

The Clydesdale horse was for many years the preferred farm work-horse and town draught horse. Big, powerful and placid they could be seen in the city delivering railway goods until the late fifties.

At Tarraby turn left and follow the narrow road for about 300 meters to cross a stile on the right into a paddock. Follow the path through the fields to Houghton and go on to the village green. This entails crossing the yard of the first house and stables. Do not be intimidated by the noisy guard dogs.

Go across the village Green, then across the main road and walk left for a short distance to enter Green Lane, turn left into Jackson Road and join a footpath on the right, halfway down the road. This footpath leads to Brunstock Beck where it passes under the motorway. Follow this track into Brunstock and continue along the minor road until you reach the B6264 road. Buses may be boarded here or at Whiteclosegate at the Nearboot Inn, for a return to Carlisle City centre. Here turn right, cross the road and a stile into a field leading you through field paths and lanes into Linstock village. Turn right and follow the minor road and paths, crossing the motorway into Rickerby village and Rickerby Park. At the cattle grid take a left path following the Hadrian's Wall Trail acorn waymarks to the Memorial suspension Bridge across the River Eden. Turn right and follow the riverside path to the Sands Centre car park.

To do the alternative 7 mile (11km) walk follow the directions above to the village green at Houghton, turn immediately left and then left again into Orchard Lane (it can be muddy) follow it left then right and continue for 150 meters until you reach a stile on the right. Cross into the field and follow the field boundary on the right to the bottom where a finger post directs you left. Continue until you reach the top right hand corner of the third field and follow the grassy lane to the main road at Greymoorhill (junction 44 on the M6 Motorway). Here cross the main road and enter a bridleway to the right of the hotel. Follow the bridleway to Parkhouse Road. Cross here into another lane between the Asda superstore car park and the industrial estate and follow the path into the northern section of Kingmoor Nature Reserve. Buses from Asda to the town centre can be boarded here – check Carlisle bus station for times.

Follow the left path to join the bed of the dismantled 'Waverley Route' railway line. Follow it and the paths behind the industrial estate until you reach the beginning of the southern section of the reserve. On the right you will see the site of the former RAF Maintenance Unit now being developed into an industrial park. Take the left track (the right track continues to the Cargo & Rockliffe Road) and follow the paths and tracks through the wood, heading south until you reach the entrance to the reserve. Here there is a car park and a board, giving information on the Nature Reserve.

Leave the reserve and turn left to join Kingmoor Road for a short distance until a stile on the right directs you into the Kingmoor Sidings Nature Reserve. Again follow the tracks south to the entrance.

The site is an ex steam locomotive depot and still shows signs of its engineering past with steel rail-track showing through the path surface. The hotel like structure on the left at the entrance is now a block of flats and was built in the days of steam, to accommodate train crews from the south.

Walk up the hill to Etterby Road and turn left. When you reach Etterby Scaur, turn right. Buses into the City centre may be boarded at the 'Redfern' pub on the left. Follow the road downhill until a footpath and sign direct you towards the River Eden. Follow this path until you reach Eden Bridge. Turn right and cross the bridge until you reach an opening on the right which leads to steps into the park and the underpass to the Sands Centre.

Railway development in Carlisle was chaotic. The Newcastle & Carlisle was the first company to come on the scene in 1836 and was soon followed by six more companies who wanted to take advantage of the city's strategic position on the west coast route between England and Scotland. Each company established its own facilities and the city quickly became a maze of engine sheds, goods depots, yards and sidings. By the late 19th century the city was one of the largest and important railway centres in Britain. Well over 100 passenger trains a day went in and out of Carlisle's magnificent Citadel Station (now simply called Carlisle) that had been built in 1847-8 to replace a number of smaller stations. There was also a huge volume of freight traffic that was interchanged between the various companies. The grouping of the old companies in 1923 into the London Midland & Scottish and The London & North Eastern resulted in some reduction, but even up until the early nineteen fifties, in British Railways days, tens of thousands of freight wagons were moving through the city each week between the various yards. Kingmoor sidings and shed originally served the Caledonian Railway, one of three pre 1923 Scottish companies that ran into Carlisle. The others were The North British Railway Company, which built and operated the 'Waverly route' through the Borders to Edinburgh and The Glasgow and South Western Railway Company. In 1963, a vast new marshalling yard covering almost three quarters of a square mile came into operation at a site to the north of the original Kingmoor sidings. It took some four years or so to construct, but its opening coincided with changes to the way rail freight was handled. and the yard never reached its full potential. It was gradually phased out of use and today little is left apart from a small modern traction depot and a few sidings used by track maintenance trains.

12 CLYDESDALES & LOCO'S

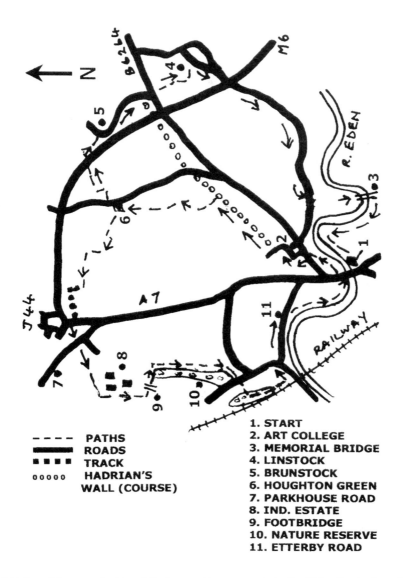

- - - - PATHS
▬▬▬ ROADS
■ ■ ■ ■ TRACK
ooooo HADRIAN'S
WALL (COURSE)

1. START
2. ART COLLEGE
3. MEMORIAL BRIDGE
4. LINSTOCK
5. BRUNSTOCK
6. HOUGHTON GREEN
7. PARKHOUSE ROAD
8. IND. ESTATE
9. FOOTBRIDGE
10. NATURE RESERVE
11. ETTERBY ROAD

13. BISHOPS, BRIDGES & CUMBRIA WAY

Five circular walks from Dalston and Rose Bridge.

Distance: From Dalston: 6, 8.5 or 11.5 miles (10, 14 or 18km).
From Rose Bridge: 2.5 or 5 miles (4 or 8km).

Maps: OS Explorer 315 (Carlisle) & Outdoor Leisure No 5 (English Lakes- North Eastern area).

Start: Dalston. The square opposite the Blue Bell Inn.
Grid Ref: NY 369 501.

Start: Rose Bridge. West side of the bridge (Cumbria Way).
Grid Ref: NY 375 469.

Parking: Dalston. The square opposite the Blue Bell Inn. If there are no spaces, use the road that leads down to the white bridge.

Parking: Rose Bridge. Across the bridge, on the road leading to Raughton Head.

There is a frequent bus service from Carlisle to Dalston. Bus times can be obtained from Carlisle Tourist Information Centre or by calling Stagecoach on 01946 63222.

To do the 6 mile (10km) walk leave the square with the Blue Bell Inn on your left and turn left along the road leading to the white bridge across the River Caldew (no through road for vehicles). The route now follows the Cumbria Way. Beyond the bridge, turn right following the millstream. Continue through the factory yard to the road. Turn right, then left towards Bridge End - ignoring the humpback bridge ahead – until you to see the Bridge End Inn on your right. Walk up the hill until a sign on the left directs you to Hawksdale and Rose Bridge. Follow this lane and the paths across the fields until you reach Hawksdale Hall and Holmhill farm. Enter the driveway to Lime House School for a short distance, until you reach a finger post on the right "to Rose Bridge". Go into the field and follow the paths through the fields and across stiles to Rose Bridge. Cross the road and go down the steps, leaving the Cumbria Way to follow the footpath to the right around the back of Rose Castle – the home of the Bishop of Carlisle. Stay on the waymarked paths until you reach the road then follow the road past the entrance to Lime House School until a fingerpost on the right directs you down a short narrow lane down to Hawksdale Farm. At the farm gate turn left to follow the footpaths and field paths to the road leading down to Bridge End. From Bridge End retrace your steps to the square in Dalston.

To extend the walk to 8.5 miles (14km). From Rose Bridge continue to follow The Cumbria Way in an approximately southwesterly direction (away from Dalston). After a mile or so you will reach Bog Bridge. Cross the river and turn right into the farm access lane. At the top of the hill, you will come to Breconhill and the magnificent trees of Foxley Henning. Staying to the left throughout, walk the minor roads into the hamlet of Raughton Head. Here turn left again to follow the road down to Rose Bridge. Beware traffic on this stretch. From Rose Bridge, follow the route back to Dalston, via Rose Castle, and Hawksdale Farm referred to in the directions for the 6 mile walk.

To extend the walk to 11.5 miles (18km) follow the directions for the 13.5km walk as far as Bog Bridge. Do not cross the bridge but continue along the riverside paths for approx 1 mile until you reach Bell Bridge. At the bridge, leave the Cumbria Way, cross the bridge onto the road and climb the hill until you reach a 'T' junction. Here turn left to join the narrow road down to Breconhill, Foxley Henning, Raughton Head and Rose Bridge**.** From Rose Bridge follow the route back to Dalston, via Rose Castle and Hawksdale Farm, referred to in the directions for the 6 mile walk.

Two short circular walks from Rose Bridge.

For the 2.5 mile (4km) circular walk start at Rose Bridge and follow the Cumbria Way in an approximately southerly direction (away from Dalston). After 800 meters or so, you will arrive at Bog Bridge. Cross the river and turn right into the farm access lane. At the top of the hill, you will reach Breconhill and the magnificent trees of Foxley Henning. Then, turning to the left at every road junction, walk the minor roads back to Rose Bridge. Beware of traffic on the road section of this walk.

For the 5 mile (8km) circular walk start at Rose Bridge and follow the Cumbria Way in an approximately southerly direction (away from Dalston). After 800 meters or so you will reach Bog Bridge. Do not cross the bridge, but continue along the riverside paths for about a further 1.5km until you come to Bell Bridge. At Bell Bridge leave the Cumbria Way, cross the bridge onto the road and climb the hill until you reach a 'T' junction. Here turn left to join the narrow road to Breconhill, Foxley Henning, Raughton Head and Rose Bridge. (At every road junction turn left). Beware of traffic on the road section of this walk.

For most of the 11th century Carlisle had been a Scottish city; then in 1092, William Rufus – son of the Conqueror- established a castle in Carlisle and a putative Border between England & Scotland at the Solway Firth. Despite the incorporation of the city into England, ecclesiastical power remained in the hands of the Scottish Bishops well into the next century. Towards the end of his life, Henry I became increasingly nervous about this seat of power headed up by the Bishop of Glasgow, who owed no allegiance to the crown of England. After all, Carlisle was a strategic part of his realm and on top of this, a likely struggle for the succession was looming.

Thus in 1133, Henry created the see of Carlisle and installed an English Bishop - Prior Adelulf. However things became decidedly tricky for the first Bishop of Carlisle, when in 1135, following the death of Henry I, King David of Scotland crossed the border and reclaimed the city. Adelulf was clearly successful in dealing with the politics of the new situation, since both the See and the Bishop survived. may also have played a part. At this period Carlisle was a place of divided loyalties and many locals joined the Scottish army. Kings and bishops were well advised to tread warily!

Rose castle is the palace of the Bishops of Carlisle and has been the scene of many notable events. In 1300, King Edward 1 and his Queen stayed here (amongst other ecclesiastical establishments) during the parliament held in Carlisle to raise funds for the 'final attack' on Scotland. This of course never happened and after Edwards death the border area was the scene of many bloody battles and skirmishes as Scotland fought for independence. In mid 1322 Robert Bruce entered England through Carlisle and amongst other things set fire to Rose castle.

13 BISHOPS BRIDGES & CUMBRIA WAY

DALSTON TO ROSE BRIDGE (LEFT). ROSE BRIDGE TO BELL BRIDGE (RIGHT)

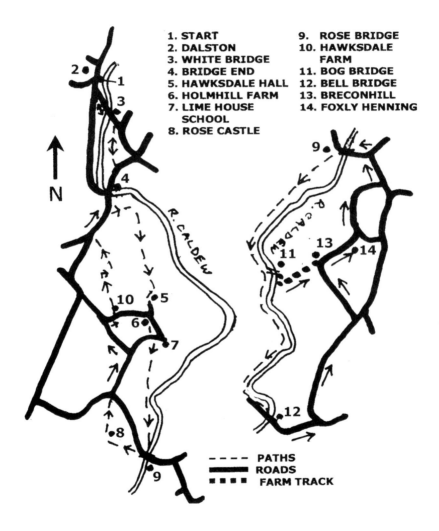

1. START
2. DALSTON
3. WHITE BRIDGE
4. BRIDGE END
5. HAWKSDALE HALL
6. HOLMHILL FARM
7. LIME HOUSE SCHOOL
8. ROSE CASTLE

9. ROSE BRIDGE
10. HAWKSDALE FARM
11. BOG BRIDGE
12. BELL BRIDGE
13. BRECONHILL
14. FOXLY HENNING

- - - - PATHS
ROADS
■ ■ ■ ■ FARM TRACK

14. CASTLE & WALL

Circular walk from Gilsland, via Thirlwall Castle and Greenhead.

Distance: 6 miles (10km).
Map: OS Explorer OL43 (Hadrian's Wall).
Start: Car park next to the school in Gilsland,
Grid Ref: NY 631 662.
Parking: Next to the school in Gilsland, Grid Ref: NY 631 662.

The car park is opposite the entrance lane to Willowford Farm and the path to Birdoswald via the new bridge.

Turn right to enter the village and right again at the junction. Almost immediately a lane on the left, signposted to Irthing House, invites you to follow the riverside footpath. At Irthing House and farm, continue ahead up and across two fields to join a metalled road. Here turn left to follow the road up and down for about ½ a mile until a finger post at a stile on the right directs you across the fields. Follow the way-marks to Curry's Rigg and Baron House to reach the Carlisle to Newcastle railway line. Walk alongside the railway for 200 meters or so before turning left to cross a footbridge onto a path that goes uphill to join the road at Woodhouse.

Here, on the high point of the walk, there are great views of the Irthing valley with its backdrop of Pennine hills to the south and Spadeadam Waste and the rolling Northumbrian landscape to the north.

Now follow the road right to reach Thirlwall Castle.

The remains of the castle have recently been repaired. Be sure to read the information board. From here, by crossing the bridge over Tipalt Burn, a linear diversion can be made to visit the Carvoran Roman Army Museum and Walltown Quarry. (There are toilets at the quarry.) This diversion is about ¾ of a mile each way. If you choose to visit the museum, simply return to the Tipalt Bridge to continue the walk.

From Tipalt Bridge, follow the path in an approximately southerly direction (the river is on your left) and cross the rail line, to the Greenhead to Gilsland Road. At the road turn right and after about

200 meters cross the road to join the Hadrian's Wall path. The remainder of the route follows the waymarked path along the line of the wall passing Chapel House and The Gap. Sections of the forward defensive ditch and the Vallum, all parts of the Hadrian's Wall World Heritage site, can be seen along this stretch. The well-marked path leads directly to the car park in Gilsland.

The initial construction of the Roman Wall is estimated to have taken ten years and it is known that three legions (the XX, the VI and the II) were involved. The legions as well as being a formidable fighting force were trained in the necessary skills of construction. No doubt the local population were 'encouraged' to do the some of the less skilled jobs! The facing stones of Hadrian's Wall are distinctly uniform in shape, being roughly 25 to 28cm wide and 15 to 18cm high. From the face they are tapered to improve bonding with the rubble and mortar core of the wall. Over the centuries much of the wall has been pulled down and the stones reused for building work. These uniform stones can be seen in churches, castles, farm buildings and field walls at numerous places close to the line of the wall. If you examine these stones you will see that the face is cut across the grain of the rock. The Romans knew full well that, although this method was more difficult and time consuming than simply splitting along the grain, it would prevent the rock from flaking as it weathered. The splendid condition of the stones almost two thousand years later is a testament to this approach. During the construction period, supplies for the legionaries would have been carted up tracks leading up from Stanegate - the road that started at Corbridge (Corstopitum) and ran eastwards to Carlisle (Luguvalium). Construction of this road was almost certainly started by the Emperor Agricola during his campaigns in the late 1st century.
A.D. This arrangement for supplying the wall garrison is thought to have continued long after the wall had been completed and that it was not until sometime in the early 3rd century that a new road directly connecting the various forts, milecastles and turrets was built. This road, now known as 'The Military Way' is still clearly visible as a broad green track immediately to the south of the wall and long sections can still be walked.

14 CASTLE & WALL

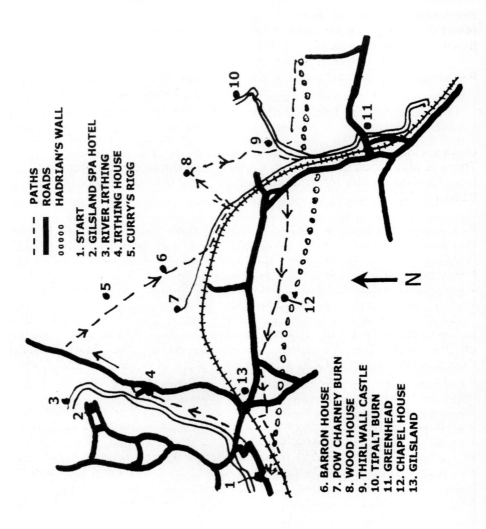

PATHS
ROADS
00000 HADRIAN'S WALL

1. START
2. GILSLAND SPA HOTEL
3. RIVER IRTHING
4. IRTHING HOUSE
5. CURRY'S RIGG

6. BARRON HOUSE
7. POW CHARNEY BURN
8. WOOD HOUSE
9. THIRLWALL CASTLE
10. TIPALT BURN
11. GREENHEAD
12. CHAPEL HOUSE
13. GILSLAND

N

15. VISTA

Circular walk from Armathwaite, through Coombs Wood & Ainstable.

Distance: 6 miles (10km).
Map: OS Outdoor Leisure No 5 (English Lakes).
Start: Bridge over River Eden at Armathwaite
Grid Reference NY 507 461.
Parking: In Armathwaite or the other side of the bridge from the village, where the road widens. Please park carefully and with consideration for the villagers.

There is a train service from Carlisle to Armathwaite on the Settle to Carlisle Line. Information can be obtained from Carlisle Station. There is also a bus service from Carlisle. Bus times can be obtained from Carlisle Tourist Information Centre or by calling Stagecoach on 01946 63222.

At the end of the bridge furthest away from the village, go down some steps and cross a stile to go below the bridge to join the riverside footpath. Now follow the waymarked woodland path along the riverbank and up through the wood, following yellow waymarks until you come to a broad, hard surface track. Continue walking upward and shortly you will arrive at an " Eden Benchmark".
"VISTA" is one of ten carved sculptures, along the banks of the Eden between Rockliffe on the Solway estuary and Mallerstang at the source of the river. The sculptures, commissioned by the East Cumbria Countryside Project (ECCP) "In a Celebration of a Very Special River"' mark the ECCP' s contribution to the millennium celebrations. Note the detail on this sculpture, a salute to walkers.
Continue up through the lovely Coombs Wood. Depending on your luck and how quietly you proceed, you may see wild animals and many species of birds in the woods and on the River. When you reach the Armathwaite to Kirkoswald road turn left. (If your time is short, you can return to Armathwaite along the road). Continue along the road for about 200 meters and turn right at a telephone box into the entrance lane to Longdales. At Longdales turn left to walk to the top of the rise and join a bridleway on the right, signed Bascodyke. Follow the bridleway to Bascodyke Head, noting that, at the first field boundary

the bridleway moves to the left of the field hedge. At the farm turn left then right before the house and then left again. Continue to follow the bridleway and the lanes to Bascodyke and Bascodyke Foot where the lane again turns right eventually to join the Ainstable road. Turn left and follow the road into the village of Ainstable, which with the exception of the church on the hill is spread out in the valley below. At the crossroads continue ahead until you reach the signpost pointing to the church on the left. Follow the road up to the church and the footpath left and around the churchyard. After the climb up from the village, a seat at the gate and seats within the porch at the church doorway are ideal for a rest.

At the bottom left hand corner of the churchyard join the path signed Towngate. Follow the wall alongside the church and then the signs and waymarks taking you left from the top left corner of the wall down to the road at Towngate Cottage. Cross the road at the footpath signed Armathwaite and again following waymarks, continue ahead across the fields with the field boundary on your right, until you reach a track. Now you will have a view of Armathwaite and the lovely valley of the River Eden. At the track, turn left and follow it down to Oaklands Cottage and the road. At the road turn left for 200 meters to join a path on the right that follows the riverbank to the bridge at Armathwaite.

The railway that crosses the tall stone viaduct on the edge of Armathwaite is the famous Settle & Carlisle Line, which came into existence as a result of the bitter rivalry between the mid-nineteenth century railway companies. The Midland Railway was prevented from reaching Carlisle and Scotland via the existing west coast line that was owned by the London & North Western Railway. To overcome the problem, the Midland proposed a new line from Settle to Carlisle. Other rivals to the LNWR supported the proposal, since they were keen to stop them creaming off the lucrative Anglo-Scottish traffic. Despite every effort of the LNWR, parliamentary assent for construction of the line was granted in 1866. At this point, the LNWR did what would now be called a 'U' turn. Realising that the new line would generate unwelcome competition the company changed its mind and offered to allow the Midland to use its tracks to Carlisle, provided of course, that the new line was never constructed. The huge estimated cost of the new line made this offer attractive and an abandonment bill was introduced into Parliament, but the original supporters would have none of it and the Midland was placed in the bizarre position of having to build a line it no longer regarded as necessary. The line opened to traffic in 1876.

15 VISTA

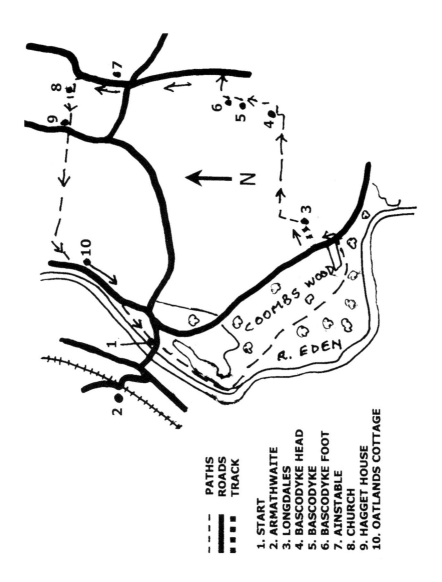

PATHS
ROADS
TRACK

1. START
2. ARMATHWAITE
3. LONGDALES
4. BASCODYKE HEAD
5. BASCODYKE
6. BASCODYKE FOOT
7. AINSTABLE
8. CHURCH
9. HAGGET HOUSE
10. OATLANDS COTTAGE

16. HIGH STAND

Two circular walks in the River Eden Valley near Armathwaite

Distance: 8 or 9 miles (13 or 14km).
Map: Outdoor Leisure No 5 (English Lakes. NE. Area).
Start: Forestry car park at High Stand. Grid Ref: NY 497 486.
Parking: Forestry car park at High Stand.

To reach High Stand take the B6263 from the M6, Junction 42, passing through Cumwhinton and turn right at Wetheral Pasture, signed Armathwaite. Continue for approximately 3 miles (5km) to the High Stand Forest Enterprise plantation on the right. Turn right after the wood and right again into the Forestry car park.

Most of this walk is over land either farmed or managed for wildlife and game, is not suitable for dogs. There are red squirrels, roe deer, badgers, and otters all in reasonable numbers. Depending on the time of year, you may see kingfishers and peregrine falcons. Take your binoculars.

Start the 8 mile (13km) walk from the car park and take the main track almost due west for ½ a mile then turn left at a path 'T' junction and head south-south-west towards Blackmoss Pool. Go through the gate to reach the crossroads. Take the right turn to Aiketgate and after about ¾ of a mile turn left at the 'T' junction. At the hamlet of Aiketgate turn left at the 'Y' junction and follow the road for about 200 meters until you will see a public footpath sign on your left directing you in a south westerly direction across a series of fields towards Armathwaite. Look well ahead for the stiles in the stone walls - this is where binoculars are useful and help you stay on the line of the right of way. Walk across farmland for about 1km and enjoy outstanding views of the surrounding countryside until you reach a lane at Hill Ends' farm. Turn left and follow the lane for about ½ a mile (ignore the first path and sign to Armathwaite that you will pass on the right) until a yellow waymark on your right directs you east across the fields. Most walks across farmland occasionally have muddy patches and this walk is no exception! Follow the field boundary to arrive at the Wetheral Pastures to Armathwaite road close to Armathwaite railway station.

You may wish to have a look around Armathwaite with its village shop, two hotels, gift shop and mill. If you do, then turn right, follow the road past the station and go down the hill into the village (about 500 meters). To continue the walk, retrace your steps to the point where the field path joined the Wetheral Pastures to Armathwaite road.

Cross the road and look for a public footpath sign to your left that directs you down a cinder track to reach the Carlisle to Settle railway line.
Steam locomotives, hauling special excursions are occasionally seen on this line. The sight and sound of the age of steam seldom fail to thrill. If you are a visitor to the district and haven't enjoyed a trip on "England's Most Scenic Rail Line", don't miss the opportunity.

Turn left and with the railway line on your right walk down until a tunnel appears under the railway. Go through the tunnel to join the Armathwaite road. Turn left and follow the road carefully until, on the left, you reach a tall, elegant viaduct – one of many on this line. Here turn right and follow the minor road past Drybeck Farm, to the riverside path that runs off the road beyond Low House. Follow the path through the narrow strip of woodland along the river through open fields, using the waymarks and signposts. At one stage the path climbs steeply up a bank then continues to follow the river from the top of the bank. Keep an eye open for where the path goes back down to the riverside and once again, your boots may be muddied. Follow the river closely. You will pass a public footpath sign to Wallace Field – do not take this path.

Continue until you come to a junction on the footpath indicated by a public footpath fingerpost. Turn left up the very steep bank and over a stile at the top and look for a "trod" (path) taking you across the rough grassland and over the railway bridge. Keeping to the fence on your left cross a short section of field and climb a stile to reach the cluster of cottages at Froddle Crook. Continue onto the Wetheral Pastures to Armathwaite road. If you've had your fill of walking for the day turn left and then right at the roads junction. This quiet road brings you back to High Stand car park.

To extend the walk to 9 miles (14km), when you reach the road near Froddle Crook, turn right onto the Wetheral Pastures to Armathwaite road and walk for about 1km until you come to another entrance (not for vehicles) into the High Stand plantation, on your left. Enter the plantation and follow the track. Eventually you will arrive at the 'T' junction mentioned in the first paragraph. Turn left and follow the track back to the car park.

High Stand plantation contains many fine Scots pine trees. Perhaps the most majestic and striking of the Northern European pines; these trees are a favoured habitat of red squirrels. At one time, the Scots pine was widely distributed over Britain, but today, only those in the Highlands of Scotland are truly wild. Elsewhere they have been cultivated. Under favourable conditions, the Scots pine can reach a hundred feet in height with a trunk up to twelve feet in girth. The characteristic profile, best seen against a background of blue sky, is the result the lower branches dying back in the early period of rapid growth.

Evidence from the pollen record shows that as the glaciers receded northwards at the end of the last ice age, Scots pine and Birch were amongst the first trees to colonise the poor rocky soils of the period. Over the next several thousand years these were joined firstly by oak and hazel and then by elms and alders. In the Eden valley there is evidence that about 3000 years ago severe soil erosion and leaching was caused by severe climate change and the removal of trees on a grand scale. Previously rich farmland became wet and acidic and almost certainly caused the local population to abandon the area.

16 HIGH STAND

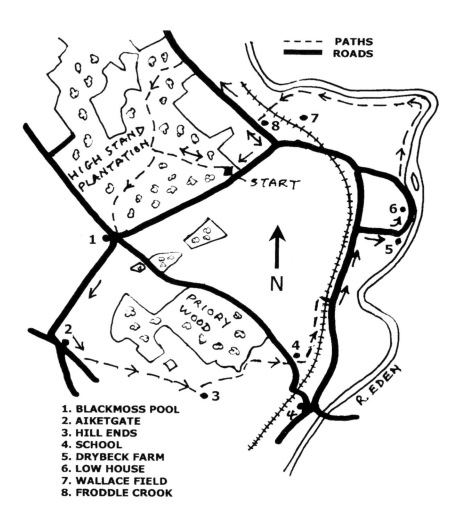

PATHS
ROADS

HIGH STAND PLANTATION

START

N

PRIORY WOOD

R. EDEN

1. BLACKMOSS POOL
2. AIKETGATE
3. HILL ENDS
4. SCHOOL
5. DRYBECK FARM
6. LOW HOUSE
7. WALLACE FIELD
8. FRODDLE CROOK

17. HEN HARRIERS & SPELTERS

Five circular walks on the Geltsdale Fells from Jockey Shield.
(Castle Carrock)

Distance: 3, 6.5, 10, 12 or 14 miles (5, 10, 16, 19 or 23km).
Maps: O.S. Explorer No 315 (Carlisle).
O.S. Outdoor Leisure OL43 (Hadrian's Wall)
Start: Jockey Shield, Grid Reference NY 558 556.
Parking: Side of the road near Jockey Shield.
(Jockey Shield is 1 mile or so to the east of Castle Carrock – follow the road to Geltsdale).

To do the 3-mile (5km) walk turn right along the high level road and enjoy the extensive views across Kings Forest of Geltsdale on the left. Follow the road for just under 1½ miles and as you approach Geltsdale House - to be seen high up to the right - turn left onto the track going downhill to a bridge crossing the River Gelt. Cross the bridge ('**A**' on map) and turn left. From here, return to Jockey Shield by following the path along the river to Low Hynam. At Low Hynam cross the River Gelt once more and walk uphill to your car.

To extend the walk to 6.5 miles (10km) cross the bridge ('**A**' on map) and turn right and follow the river to The 'North West Water' pumping station. Geltsdale is a catchment area for the Castle Carrock Reservoir, which supplies water to Carlisle. Once past the buildings take a half left turn uphill to follow the track to a 'T' junction on the bridleway. Here, turn left and follow the bridleway to a bridge crossing Old Water Burn. Cross the bridge and continue uphill for approximately 300 meters. Go through a gate and look out for and turn left on to a path climbing the side of the fell. Soon the path joins a track. Turn left here and now there by is some truly delightful walking with short, soft grass underfoot and superb views northwards to the Solway Firth and Scottish hills beyond. After 1½ miles take the track going downhill to the left from point ('**B**' on map), towards a derelict house - Gairs, formerly the home of the Geltsdale mine manager. This track leads directly to Low Hynam Bridge, Jockey Shield and your car, completing the 6.5 mile walk.

To extend the walk to 10 miles (16 km) do not go down track ('**B**' on map) to Gairs, but continue along the grassy track, skirting Brown fell, towards the hamlet of Howgill ('**C**' on map). From Howgill, take the track northwards until you reach a junction at Tortie where, by turning left, you can reach Forest Head with it's massive lime kilns and quarries. Notice the line of the disused railway track on the left as you head for Tortie. From Forest Head, take the road straight ahead and after 1km you will see a house set back from the road on your left. Go through the gate and walk ahead on to an old track uphill, passing quarry workings to your left. Do not enter the quarry. At the top of the hill, turn right at a fence, follow it for a few metres and go through a gate. The track downhill, which becomes more obvious as you progress, bends to the right and comes to another gate. Go through the gate and continue downhill along the lane. On reaching some woods on the left look out for a footpath sign pointing left for Low Hynam. Follow this path downhill to Low Hynam Bridge. When you reach the bridge, cross it and go uphill to Jockey Shield.

To extend the walk to 12 miles (19km) at Howgill ('**C**' on map) go through a gate leading to the path along Howgill Beck and eventually past a pair of derelict houses on your left – Stagsike – until you reach a narrow road on the left. Go left along this road to Thorn then left again to Tortie and Forest Head. From Forest Head take the road straight ahead and after 1km you will see on your left, a house set back from the road. Go through the gate on to an old uphill track that passes this house and eventually passes quarry workings to your left. Do not enter the quarry. At the top of the hill, turn right at a fence, follow it for a few metres and go through a gate. The track downhill, which becomes more obvious as you progress, bends to the right and comes to another gate. Go through the gate and continue downhill along the lane. On reaching some woods on the left look out for a footpath sign pointing left for Low Hynam. Follow this path downhill to Low Hynam Bridge. When you reach the bridge, cross it and go uphill to Jockey Shield.

If you have the energy to extend the walk to the full 14 miles (23km) leave Howgill ('**C**' on map) and follow Howgill Beck along the road past 'Stagsike' and past Tarn House Farm beyond which the route becomes a footpath. Tindale Tarn can be seen on the left. Soon you will reach a group of bungalows and caravans beyond them turn left down and up to Tindale.

Tindale has relics of the heyday of coal mining, lime burning, spelter working and zinc refining. The zinc ore was imported and local lime and coal was used in the processing.

At Tindale, look out for yellow waymarks on your left inviting you through a gate on to the open fell – Tarnhouse Rigg. Take this route and stay in the same direction for 1¼ miles - the Tarn can be seen down on the left - until you reach Thorn. At Thorn, cross a stile and join a narrow road. Follow this road for about 1km until you reach another gate.   Go through this gate and follow the hard surface track almost opposite for ½ a mile, passing a set of three limekilns on the left, to reach the road at Forest Head. Take the road straight ahead and after 1km you will see a house set back from the road on your left. Go through the gate and walk ahead on to an old track uphill passing quarry workings to your left. Do not enter the quarry. At the top of the hill, turn right at a fence, follow it for a few metres and go through a gate. The track downhill, which becomes more obvious as you progress, bends to the right and comes to another gate. Go through the gate and continue downhill along the lane. On reaching some woods on the left look out for a footpath sign pointing left for Low Hynam. Follow this path downhill to Low Hynam Bridge. When you reach the bridge, cross it and go uphill to Jockey Shield.

Tindale is an alternative starting point for all these walks. There is parking space just above the green (Grid Reference NY 618 593). Tindale is reached from the road between Hallbankgate and Midgeley. You can do a circular walk around Tindale Tarn by following the bridleway across Tarnhouse Rigg to Thorn then turning left to join the road to Tarn House and the ongoing footpath back to Tindale.

All these walks can be varied according to time available and your fitness capability. Enjoy this wonderful area and don't forget your binoculars.

Geltsdale is a fascinating collection of low fells, tarns, mining and industrial remains, swift flowing streams, rare birds and a wildlife/nature reserve. The reserve was enlarged in 2002 by the purchase, of Tarn House Farm & Tindale Tarn by the RSPB. The farmland, including the fellside above is very extensive and the purchase, designed to foster the survival and breeding of rare bird species – Hen Harrier, Black Grouse, Curlew - has delighted conservationists.

17 HEN HARRIERS & SPELTERS
ROUTES FOR 3, 6.5 & 10 MILE WALKS

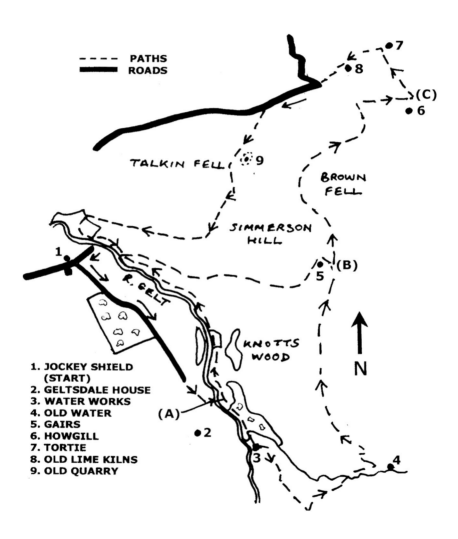

PATHS
ROADS

7
8
(C)
6
TALKIN FELL 9
BROWN
FELL
SIMMERSON
HILL
(B)
5
1
R. GELT
KNOTTS
WOOD
N

1. JOCKEY SHIELD
   (START)
2. GELTSDALE HOUSE
3. WATER WORKS
4. OLD WATER
5. GAIRS
6. HOWGILL
7. TORTIE
8. OLD LIME KILNS
9. OLD QUARRY

(A)
2
3
4

17 HEN HARRIERS & SPELTERS
EXTENSIONS TO 12 OR 14 MILES

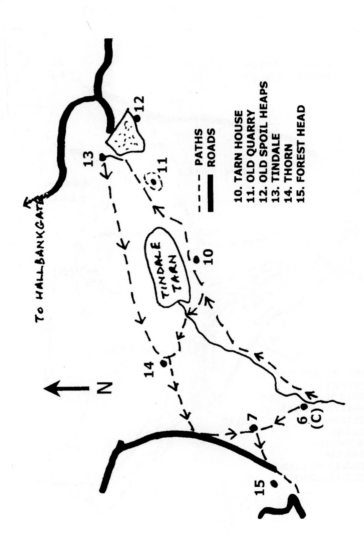

- - - - PATHS
▬▬▬ ROADS

10. TARN HOUSE
11. OLD QUARRY
12. OLD SPOIL HEAPS
13. TINDALE
14. THORN
15. FOREST HEAD

To HALLBANKGATE

TINDALE TARN

N